# 50 OBJECT STORIES FOR CHILDREN

# 50 OBJECT STORIES FOR CHILDREN

## CHARLOTTE COOPER

**BAKER BOOK HOUSE**
Grand Rapids, Michigan 49516

ISBN: 0-8010-2523-0

*Second printing, September 1988*

Printed in the United States of America

Unless otherwise identified, Scripture quotations in this volume are from
the New International Version, ©1978 by New York International Bible
Society. Used with permission of The Zondervan Corporation. Scripture
quotations identified RSV are from the Revised Standard Version of the
Bible, ©1972 by Thomas Nelson, Inc.

Ideas for ''The Hurt in the Heart'' were developed by Linda Patterson.

To the children of Lages

# Contents

# Introduction:
## *Telling the Story*

Storytelling is an old and honorable human activity. It was the means for explaining who we were and what that meant long before we had the written word.

It was an important activity of Bible times. Certainly the very earliest stories were told before they were ever written down. The Holy Spirit guided and preserved those words as well as the written ones. Around ancient fires, with darkness flickering all around, those who had trusted God and walked with him, told stories of the faithfulness of the Lord God, his care for his creation, his love for his children.

Jesus, telling truth that burned, truth that nourished, truth that relieved the burden of sin and eternal death, used stories so simple that they could be understood by everyone who heard him.

In the three or four minutes that the "children's time" takes, it is possible to pass some vital truths to children.

The first truth we tell them is that they are important, and they have a place in the worshiping community. We express that by having a time and place for them in the midst of the serious adult business of the Sunday-morning service. We express it by looking into their faces, waiting for them to find a place. The extra twenty seconds that it takes to wait for a straggling child to come and find a spot to sit seems very long, with a church full of adults waiting, but it says to that child in a powerful way, "You are important. Of course I will wait for you!"

I have not tried to tell Bible stories (except for the triumphal entry for Palm Sunday and "Good News for Rotten Kids," part of the prodigal son story). Instead, I have tried to make a single point, using an object or an experience that is already familiar to most children. I hope that later, when they handle a flashlight or a quarter, when they pull on their sneakers or their raincoats, these objects will remind them of a Savior who knows them so well that he knows the number of hairs on their heads.

Some points are made many times in many ways. This is both educationally and scripturally sound. Some authorities believe it takes as many as forty exposures before new learning is assimilated. Scripture tells us many times, in many contexts, to put God first in trust and focus; it tells us many times to confess our sins and be forgiven; it tells us again and again that we are loved beyond measure. Repetition is okay; in fact, it is necessary.

When I told these stories, I did not look at the adult

congregation, nor did I make any special effort to have them hear me. I would have become distracted and even self-conscious if I had. I was aiming at the child (not even the "children" but *the* "child") to whom God wanted to speak. I could not possibly know all of his specific purposes for them. I know he intended to bless them, and that I needed to be faithful in conveying to them Bible truths week by week.

Nevertheless, adults did enjoy the children's time and often responded to the truths presented there. Certainly the child within each adult is precious, and sometimes that old and hidden child was touched.

Once we had started, we learned we could not say:

"There will be no children's sermon today," whatever the reason, and expect the children to file out to children's church. The day we tried it, nothing happened. Then one child wandered up to the front and looked around, bewildered. Finally, I went up to the front (along with the choir director, who is also the local elementary-school principal), and we invited the children to come up. When they came, I led them out, but they were disappointed, and we never tried to do it again.

The words of these small children's sermons may sometimes seem sparse. They are meant to be. You are not up there alone; you have invited any child who wants to come. It is the same invitation Jesus gave, and you now have the matchless privilege of telling them that Jesus did that, that he does it now. Little by little, line upon line, you can tell them who Jesus is, how he is the way to the Father, and that he loves them. It is appropriate to give the children the opportunity of participating, of asking, of answering.

These are sermon starters suitable for children's

time in a regular service, or for a Sunday school class, or Vacation Bible School, or any other occasion involving young children. Use the names of real people if you know someone who illustrated the point you are trying to make. They can be given just as they are written. (They are written very nearly as they were given.) If you do this, read them over several times, changing any words or phrases that are not comfortable. You will need to read the Scripture that is given and understand it thoroughly. *It is not always workable to read it to the children*. If you do, take your Bible up there with you, open it, but have the Scripture memorized and *say* it to them, looking into their faces as you do so.

In the same way, *tell* the story. If you read it, much will be lost. Telling is powerful in a way that reading is not.

Some children really want to talk! I got a rash of "know what?" "Save the 'know whats' for later," I would say, and sail right on. Sometimes it was necessary to insist, "*I* need to talk now!" but moving swiftly was the most effective. Occasionally, I followed the children into children's church to complete a conversation with a child. On one of these occasions, Laura asked Jesus to come into her heart. She was persistent in wanting to do this, and though she was only seven, seemed to grasp what it meant. I led her through a prayer right there, but it was clearly not settled, so I followed the children out, and we completed our transaction with eternity in the hall outside.

Here, then, are fifty stories for you to use. They are pebbles dropped into a pool. One alone is not much, but week after week, one after another, they will affect the very configuration of the pool into which they fall. You will not know how far the ripples spread. It is a small moment on any given Sunday morning; but it is no small effort in the kingdom of God.

As you watch human beings, all three or four feet tall, appear from behind the pews and the large bodies that have concealed them (and blocked their view), as you watch them come up the aisle, eagerly or shyly, and find a spot to sit comfortably beside you in the midst of the church (both the building and the gathering) you will be moved. As they come to a welcoming adult, who smiles and waits and makes sure there is a place for them, they will be in a position to hear that they are welcome also in the family of our Lord Jesus Christ. May it be a blessing all around!

> "Whom will he teach knowledge,
>     and to whom will he explain the message?
> Those who are weaned from the milk . . .
> For it is precept upon precept, . . .
>     line upon line, line upon line,
>     here a little, there a little."
>
> Isaiah 28:9,10 (RSV)

# 1

## The Name in the Palm of His Hand

**Opportunity:** Whenever there are some children you don't know.

**Materials:** A fine tip marker or a ball-point pen.

**Point:** God knows each of us by name, he will never forget.

**Scripture:** Isaiah 49:15, 16

> Can a mother forget the baby at her breast
>   and have no compassion on the child she has
>   borne?
> Though she may forget,
> I will not forget you!
> See, I have engraved you on the palms of my
>   hands. . . .

*(As the children come up, call one aside—an older child—and whisper that you would like to write his or her name on the palm of your hand. Do so, not showing it to the others.)*

I know some of you. I see some of you at school, [*Name two or three children.*] Some of you have been to my house. I would like the rest of you to tell me your names, and I will see how many I can remember.

(*Have them tell you their names.*)

Now let's see how many I can remember.

(*Repeat as many as you can. The story depends on your forgetting some of them!*)

I remember you are _____ and _____ and _____ and this is _____, but I can't remember your name, or yours, or yours.

Here is one name I know for sure; that is Phillip. Do you know why I remember?

(*Open your hand and show them the name written there.*)

Phillip's name is written on my hand.

You know, your name is very important. It says who you are. The Bible says that God knows your name and he will never forget it. In fact, it says that it is written on his hand. *Your name!* That is how important you are to God.

Let's pray:

"Lord Jesus, we thank you that you know each one of us here so well. Thank you that you know each one of our names and will never forget them. *Amen.*"

# 2

# A Letter from Dad

**Occasion:** Watch for a Dad (or Mom) who has to go away on a trip (not someone who is leaving permanently!). Ask that parent to write a short letter to their child, one that can be shared in church. When the time comes, you will need to ask the child's permission to read the letter. If the answer is *no*, honor it and go on to describe the type of thing it might say.

**Point:** God has left messages for us in the Bible.

**Materials:** The letter and a Bible.

**Scripture:** John 14:1–21 (Scripture in story is paraphrased.)

Robby's dad had to leave yesterday. He'll be away for a week or so. (*Mention briefly:* "He had business" or "He had to get his cast changed at the hospital.")

He left a letter for his son. I have it right here.

What do you think he might say in his letter?

(*Some possible answers:* "Be good . . . I love you . . . I'll be back soon.")

Robby, could we read the letter? You come over here by me, and we'll read it together.

(*Robby said yes. If not, I would not have read the letter, but just gone on.*)

It says:

Dear Robby,

You know I have to go away for a little while. Be a good boy while I am gone. Help Mom with the chores.

Keep practicing jogging, and when I come back we'll go jogging together again. You're my best boy.

I love you,
DADDY

Thank you, Robby. That's a special letter and it belongs to you to keep.

We have letters from Jesus. They say the same things Robby's daddy says [*open Bible*]:

"I'm going away for a little while, and I'll send my Holy Spirit to comfort you while I'm gone.

"I'm coming back someday.

"If you love *me*, do what I have told you, love each other.

"I love you."

These are our letters from Jesus. He wants us to know that he loves us, too. They are here for us to read anytime we want to.

# 3

## The Parable of the Lost Puppy

**Occasion:** When there is a new, quiet, puppy available. (*You can't really bring a lamb into church, but you can bring a puppy, if it's very small and quiet and you have something plastic and paper-lined to bring it in. I came in late and sat in the back with the ushers until the time for the children's story. Immediately after, I took it out of the church. Kittens don't work. They have a tendency to scratch and to escape.*)

**Point:** Jesus cares for the small and helpless, including children.

**Materials:** Puppy, in container that conceals and contains it.

**Scripture:** Luke 15:3–7

(*Take out the puppy. Let the children touch it.*)

Isn't it small?
It belongs to my next-door neighbor. They watch

him very carefully. They don't let him go off by himself at all. What would happen if he got in the street? ("He could get run over.")

What if he got loose in the field? ("A larger animal, a cow or a donkey might hurt him.")

Jesus says we are like little lost animals, like a puppy or a lamb. He needs to watch over us, to care for everyone. If one person gets far away from him, or if someone doesn't even know about him, do you know what he does? He goes to look for that one. Sometimes he sends one of us to look. He wants to bring each person safely into his care.

Let's put the puppy back in here, and we'll all go out that door.

*(Don't try to have a prayer. They will all be looking at the puppy. Don't tell the puppy's name or do anything to encourage sentimentality. The object is to understand that the puppy is helpless and needs to be cared for. If children's church can accommodate it, you may want to take it in there. Otherwise, arrange to have it out of the way of the worship service and in safe care elsewhere.)*

# 4

# What Do You Think You'll Get?

**Opportunity:** Anytime.

**Materials:** Wear a jacket with two generous pockets. Have some little pebbles or stones in one pocket and have some M&Ms or other small soft candy in the other. Be sure to have enough for each child!

**Point:** We can ask God for anything: he will only give us good gifts. The Holy Spirit is one of his best gifts.

**Scripture:** Luke 11:11–13

Have you ever given anyone a present? What have you given them? What do you think is a good gift?

(*Children will have many answers. Take a minute to let them tell you.*)

Do your parents ever give you things?

(*Again, children will have many answers. Move right on.*)

If you asked your father for a hot dog, would he ever give you a snake instead?

("No.")

If you ask your mother for a cookie, will she give you a rock?

("No, she doesn't let me put rocks in my mouth.")

The Bible says that even though we are not always perfect people, we do know how to give good presents to people we love. Even more, God, who is always good, just loves to give us good gifts. If we ask him, he will give us his own Holy Spirit to be with us all the time. And that is a *very good* gift.

I have something to give you. Let me see. In this pocket I have some stones. I picked them up in my driveway. Do you think that might be it?

("No.")

How about this pocket. (*Hold up a couple of M&Ms.*)

("Yes, that's it.")

(*Give each child an M&M as they go out to children's church. Have a few extra; there are some adults who need M&Ms too!*)

# 5

## Weeds

**Opportunity:** Anytime of the year that you can pull a big weed.

**Point:** Sin is deeply rooted. It gets in the way of growth.

**Materials:** A paper sack with a small weed, a weed with a long tap root, and a packet of small seeds inside.

**Scripture:** Matthew 5:29:

> If your right eye causes you to sin, gouge it out and throw it away. It is better for you to lose one part of your body than for your whole body to be thrown into hell.

*(This Scripture is for you to consider. Do not use this imagery with children. It will frighten and confuse them. It is meant for adults. The idea of the root of the weed conveys the meaning without threatening the child's body.)*

I've been digging in my garden. I'm getting

ready to plant these [radish or other seeds]. They are going to be [radishes], when they grow, but the seeds are very small.

There are a lot of weeds in my garden, and I've been pulling them out so the seeds can grow.

Most of them are easy to pull out. (*Show the small one.*)

When I pulled this one, though, the top just started to break off. I couldn't get it out. I had to go and get my shovel and dig it out. It had a root too deep for me to pull. (*Show a long-rooted weed such as a big healthy dandelion.*)

Sin is like a weed. It's pretty easy to stop some things—to say sorry or to stop hitting or teasing. But some sin is like this big root; you can pull the top off, but the root of the sin is still there. It's too deep to get out by yourself.

What can you do about a sin that goes deep?

("Ask Jesus to take it out.")

or Who could take care of it?

("Jesus could.")

That's why he came, isn't it? To take care of our sin. Let's pray:

"Lord, thank you that you can take the sin out of our lives, so that good things can grow there. It's so good to belong to you, and we love you. *Amen.*"

# 6

## In God We Trust

**Occasion:** Anytime, but especially if something a little scary, like the first day of school, is coming up.

**Point:** We do trust in God, each one specifically and for specific things.

**Materials:** A quarter.

**Scripture:** Isaiah 12:2

Does anyone have to do anything this week that makes them kind of nervous?

This quarter has a message on it. (*Turn the coin over in your hand and hold it up.*) I don't think other countries usually do, but in our country, the USA, our coins all have this message on them.

One time a little girl I knew had to go to the dentist. She wasn't afraid, but she was a little nervous.

Her mom said, "I'll fix your hair especially nice, and you can wear your new sneakers and your new

T-shirt, and I'll give you something special to carry in your hand.''

So the next morning she got ready. She got her hair all fixed. She put on her new sneakers and her new shirt. Then her mom gave her a quarter.

She said:

''You just hold this in your hand and remember what it says and you'll be just fine.''

And she did and she was.

Anybody know what it says? (*Somebody will know!* ''In God We Trust.'')

(*After church I waited, ready to give the quarter to the first adult who told me he or she needed it. Someone did say that. It was a person who was a boss of many people. He needed to be reminded to trust in God, too.*)

# 7

## Sleeping Over

**Occasion:** If someone dies.

**Point:** Jesus has a special place, a good place, for the person.

**Materials:** None.

**Scripture:** John 14:1–3

One time, a little boy I know was talking to God, just before he went to sleep. His mom (that was me) was there and he said:

"Mom, I really know something. Someday we're going to see Jesus, and we're going to sleep over."

That's what _____ is doing. He's sleeping over. His parents and his sister and his friends are really sad because they wanted him to stay here. They hoped that he would stay with them for a long time and then go to Jesus when he was very old. But for _____ it's okay.

Jesus promised to make a place that would be just right for him, and he's just fine. Jesus has a place waiting for his mom and dad, too, and it will be ready for them and for all of us who trust in him.

Let's pray:

"Thank you, Jesus, for taking care of _____. We still miss him, but we know he is sleeping over with you, and that makes us happy for him. *Amen.*"

*(Talk of dying is often avoided with children, but they need to know too, what the promises are. To avoid talking about a death in their circle of family and friends only leaves disquieting uncertainties. Let us share Jesus' promises with them!)*

# 8

## Raincoats Aren't Enough

**Occasion:** Rainy season.

**Point:** We need special protection in the world.

**Materials:** A raincoat.

**Scripture:** Ephesians 6:10–18

I wore my raincoat today. Did you bring yours to church with you? I thought it was going to rain. This is a good raincoat. It covers me from the top of my head [*show the hood*] all the way down to my knees. It keeps all the rain off. It has a good belt that I can pull nice and tight.

I brought my rain hat, too [*if you didn't have a hood*]. It keeps my head dry. [*Pull it on.*] I have some boots that keep the water and mud off my feet. Do you have boots?

(*The children will enjoy telling you about their boots.*)

27

We have to have this kind of protection in rainy weather.

The Bible says that when we belong to Jesus, we have some special protection too. You can't see it, but it's there, so that if anything that would be bad for you comes along, you'll be protected.

The Bible says that righteousness, that is, being right with God, is like a coat or a raincoat—it covers us over.

Truth, that is, the things that Jesus said, is like a belt, to pull the coat tight around us.

The good news that we can be friends with God is like a pair of good boots, to protect us wherever our feet take us. And to protect our heads—all the things we see and hear and think—we have the fact that we are saved. It's almost like a football helmet.

So, when you put on your raincoat this week, and your rain hat and your boots, remember that you are already wearing a special protection for the *inside* of you—one that God himself has given you.

Let's pray:

"Thank you, Lord, for giving us special protection from anything that might hurt us. We know that we are your children and that you love us. *Amen.*"

*(This seemed a little remote for very young children, but there were older children in the group as well. This is for them! The imagery is direct and scriptural, ready to be recollected at a later time. A lawyer in the congregation liked it!)*

# 9

## Lifting Weights

**Opportunity:** Anytime. If a dad or big brother of one of the children lifts weights or works out, ask to borrow their weights.

**Point:** Trust, faith in Jesus, grows stronger when it is exercised.

**Materials:** An all-in-one-piece weight. They come in 5 pound or 3 kilo (6.6 pounds) weights.

**Scripture:** Philippians 4:13

I can do everything through him who gives me strength.

Can you lift this? Hold your arm out and try it.

(*Let several children try.*)

Peter uses this to make his arms stronger. After he broke his arm, he used it every day to build up the muscle in that arm again. If you use it every day, pretty soon your muscles get hard and very strong, so that you can lift even bigger weights.

This is called a *curl*. [*Show the children how to bring your hand to your shoulder, holding the weight*.] Peter can do this 150 times, but I can only do it a few times.

Trusting God is like lifting weights. In order to be strong in faith, you have to keep practicing. You have to keep on trusting God for little things, so you will be able to trust him for big things.

The Bible tells us to be strong in the Lord and in his mighty power.

Jesus said to his friends:

"Be faithful in little and I will make you faithful in much."

So, just like building strong muscles takes practice, in the same way you will grow stronger in Jesus every time you practice trusting him.

# 10

## Somebody's Own
## Dear Child

**Opportunity:** Watch for someone who has a little child and also does ceramics.

**Point:** Jesus is God's own dear child, not his creation.

**Materials:** Ceramic figure, preferably made by the mother or father, a photograph of the child (a particular child, whose photograph it is). A baby can also be used, and in fact, ceramic figures of babies are easier to find.

**Scripture:** John 3:13–16

This is a little ceramic figure. David's mother made it herself. She poured the clay into a mold, and then when it was dry, she took it out and trimmed it. She put it in a special oven to bake it hard. Then she painted it and baked it again.

(*If the child interrupts you with the correct terms, "kiln" and "fired," acknowledge this with appreciation.*)

This is . . . ? (*Hold up the picture of David.*)

Where is David? He's the real one, isn't he? The one who is alive and breathing and himself.

What would happen if I lost the photograph? Or dropped the figure and broke it?

("David's mother would be unhappy, but not very.")

What if anything ever happened to the boy? If he got hurt?

("That would be terrible" . . . "They would be *very* upset.")

David is *very* important isn't he? He's their own dear boy, and they take very special care of him. Don't they David?

(*David nods eagerly; he feels special and loved.*)

When God sent us a Savior, he didn't send us someone he had made [*hold up the figure*]. He didn't send us a picture of someone special [*hold up the photo*]. He sent us his own, his real son.

Even though the world was a dangerous place for a little baby to be born, he sent us Jesus just that way. Jesus grew up to die on the cross, and God the Father knew that that would happen. He let his son come to rescue us.

I think he must love us a lot to do that, don't you?

# 11

## Good News for Bad Kids, or, The Really Rotten Kid

**Opportunity:** Anytime.

**Point:** God loves people, even bad people, and he welcomes them when they approach him.

**Materials:** None needed.

**Scripture:** Luke 15:11–24

Who of you always tries to do the right thing? To be a good kid? To help out and obey the rules? (*Kids raise hands.*)

Lots of you do, but some people don't. We all know people who are really naughty. (*Be sure to stop any identifications!*)

Jesus told in this story about a man who had two sons. One son *always* helped out. He *always* obeyed the rules. He was really a good son.

The other one *never* helped if he could get out of it. He broke all kinds of rules. His mother and father were always worrying about him.

When he grew up he said to his father:

"Just give me that money you were saving for my college. I want to spend it *my* way. I don't care what you were planning."

The father didn't want to do that, but after a while he did.

The son went out and just wasted it. He didn't get a job. He just fooled around. After a while the money was gone. He got hungry and he had no place to live.

He thought about his father's house. He decided to go back and ask his father to take him on as a hired man. At least he would have something to eat and a place to sleep.

But while he was still a long way off, his father saw him. What do you think he did to such a bad son? (*Pause for comments.*)

His father ran to him and threw his arms around him! He hugged him and he kissed him!

The son said, "I am so ashamed. I have done everything wrong. I don't even deserve to be your son anymore."

But the father said, "You are my son and I love you! I thought you were dead, but here you are alive! We are going to celebrate!"

And they did.

Jesus told us, "This is how God loves you." Even if you are the really rotten kid, he is waiting for you because he loves you!

(*This was prepared with a particular child in mind. He didn't come that morning, but someone else was listening. A middle-aged man, someone with position and power in the community, drew me aside after and told me it had been for him. I could not know whose heart God was planning to speak to in that story.)*

# 12

## The Hurt in the Heart

**Occasion:** Anytime.

**Point:** People who are rude and mean often have a hurt inside.

**Materials:** None.

**Scripture:** Proverbs 18:13–15

> He who answers before listening—
>   that is his folly and his shame.
> A man's spirit sustains him in sickness,
>   but a crushed spirit who can bear?
> The heart of the discerning acquires knowledge,
>   the ears of the wise seek it out.

Have you ever had a little stone in your shoe? Did it hurt? Did you walk funny until you took it out? What about a real hurt on your foot?

Did you ever bite your tongue really bad? Did you talk differently until it healed? What about this child [*name him or her*] with his/her teeth out? Does it change the way that person sounds?

So, a hurt on your foot will change the way you walk, and a hurt in your mouth may change the way you talk.

What about a hurt in your heart?

What if your friend is up to bat, and he strikes out, and you go to him and say, "Good try. Better luck next time."

What might he say? ("He might say, 'Get out of here.'")

Yes, he might say something like that because he was feeling bad.

So sometimes when a person acts funny or even mean, it could be because they have a hurt inside. What can a friend do then? ("A friend would still stay around them". . . ."They would wait for them to get over it.")

Yes, it is still important to be his friend. Will you think about that this week if someone says something rude to you?

(*This is something most children have not considered before. Their responses are important. Your goal is to help them to think of what the other person might be feeling. It is a very open-ended children's sermon, without an exact ending. If it is effective, you may never know, but the Lord can use it to make some of his children more like himself in loving others.*)

# 13

## Palm Sunday

**Opportunity:** Palm Sunday. This alone of the stories is not a parable or an object lesson. It is just the telling of the events of the triumphal entry of Jesus into Jerusalem. It has a ''grown-up'' theme which children badly need. They are told a lot of playful and even silly things about Easter. Let us honor them with the truth about the events that led to the best of all surprises: the resurrection.

**Materials:** None.

**Point:** Jesus really was a King. He chose to come on a little donkey, into his city.

**Scripture:** Luke 19:28–40

Have you ever seen a mother donkey with her little colt? The colt likes to stay close beside the mother.

Once there was a little donkey, tied beside its mother, in a town nearby where Jesus was staying.

The little donkey was almost grown, almost big enough to be ridden but, as a matter of fact, no one had yet ridden on it.

Two strangers came along and started to untie the colt and his mother. The people who lived there said:

"Hey! Where do you think you're going with those donkeys?"

The men just said:

"The master needs them."

The donkeys' owners knew that the men meant Jesus, and they said it was all right.

The men took the two donkeys, the mother and the colt, to Jesus. He was waiting by the side of the road. They put their coats and their capes on the backs of the donkeys to make a smooth place to sit. Jesus got on the colt.

Crowds of people came to watch as they went along the road. They were shouting and cheering. They were saying:

"Hooray! Jesus is coming! He is the King! He is the King!"

Some people even put their coats down on the street so that Jesus wouldn't have to ride over the dirty cobblestones. They put green leaves and branches down to make it nice.

There was a lot of noisy cheering, but the little donkey and his mother just went quietly along, carrying Jesus into the city.

Pretty soon, some scary and terrible things were going to happen to Jesus, but he knew about them and he knew that he would win. *He* knew that he really *was* the King, and that day, when he rode into the city on the little donkey, all the people knew it, too.

(*The triumphal entry is hard to present to little children because it involves many complex factors, and a child of four or five, especially in the excitement of coming up in the front of the church, can only deal with one or two in those brief moments.*

*I chose to make the points that Jesus was a real King and that he rode on a little donkey.*

*We had palm branches to give out. They were placed on a small round table near the spot where the children would gather. To insure that we wouldn't have palm branches scattered hither and yon, I enlisted the help of a teenager, who went to the front when I did, and simply sat on the floor between the children and the palms.*

*At the end of the talk, she helped me to pass them out. I really needed her! The children were fascinated by the palms. Instead of saying, "Don't touch!" we arranged to give one to each child as they left the sanctuary for children's church.*)

# 14

## In a Mirror Darkly

**Opportunity:** Camping season.

**Point:** Now we understand Jesus imperfectly, but someday we will actually see him.

**Materials:** Metal camp mirror.

**Scripture:** 1 Corinthians 13:12

> Now we see but a poor reflection; then we shall see face to face. Now I know in part; then I shall know fully, even as I am fully known.

W hat do you think Jesus looks like?
(*Let the children answer.*)

There are no photographs. The pictures that we see are somebody's guesses.

The Bible says that we can tell what Jesus is like but not very clearly.

It's like this. (*Bring out the camping mirror.*)

This is a mirror to take camping. It won't break. It's made of steel. I can see my face in it [*turn it so that children can see, too*] but it's kind of foggy looking. It's not nearly as good as just looking right at you.

That's how it is with Jesus. We can tell what he is like but not real well.

But one of these days, when he comes back, or when we go to meet him, we will actually get to see him face to face, you and I, and he will be looking back at us.

Won't that be exciting?

# 15

## Favorite Person

**Occasion:** Anytime.

**Point:** Each one of us is Jesus' favorite person.

**Materials:** None.

**Scripture:** 1 John 1:4–9

Do you have a favorite person?

Who would it be? ("My friend is Amy"..."My mom is my best friend.")

Do you know who my favorite friend is? ("Is it God?") Well, yes, but besides God...My favorite friend is Chaplain Cooper, and Peter, and...my mother, and...I really like Chantel's mother. I guess I have more than one favorite person.

Do you know who God's favorite person is? It's you...and you...and *you*! God has more than one favorite person too.

The Bible says:

"This is how God shows his love among us; he sent his one and only Son into the world that we might live through him" (1 John 4:9).

Do you like being God's favorite person?

It's pretty nice.

Let's pray:

"Father, thank you that we are each so special to you. We love you, too. *Amen.*"

# 16

## Uniforms

**Opportunity:** Whenever someone has a new uniform they are proud to wear. It can be in the fall, when the Cub Scouts and the Brownies initiate new members, or when someone gains a new rank in scouting, or when a big brother comes home proudly wearing a new military uniform. (*Ask around so that you will know ahead of time.*)

**Point:** We are covered with Jesus' righteousness, the covering that indicates that we belong to him.

**Materials:** The uniform(s) that the congregation is currently aware of.

**Scripture:** Isaiah 61:10
Revelation 3:4, 5

Some of you are new Cub Scouts. I saw you wearing your uniforms last night. Some of you older scouts had a special scarf to wear. It told everyone

45

who saw you in your uniform that you belong to the Boy Scouts.

How did it feel to wear that uniform?

("Proud, really excited.")

Last night General Smith said that he liked wearing his uniform when he was a Boy Scout. [*Mention which-ever adult would be significant.*]

Did you know that the Bible says that when we come to heaven to live with Jesus there, we will have a special outfit to wear? Do you know that it is?

It's called a *robe of righteousness*. It's sparkling white and it's made just for you, to fit you exactly. You can't see yours now, but if you belong to Jesus, you already have one. You'll get it in heaven. Like a uniform, it shows that you belong there.

Do you know how you get it?

You get it when you believe in Jesus and you ask him to forgive you whatever is wrong. *He* has one for everyone who belongs to him.

When you join the scouts you get a scout uniform, right?

When you join Jesus in heaven, he has a special outfit for you to wear there, too.

# 17

## The Day the Sun Was Darkened

**Opportunity:** When there is a dramatic natural event. In this case it was an eclipse. If you have recently experienced a flood or a mighty storm, use it as you talk to children about the greatness of God.

**Point:** The sun grew dark (really dark, not like the dimness of the eclipse) when Jesus, the Light of the World, was dying for our sakes.

**Materials:** A brown or black sheet of paper with a pinhole in it.

**Scripture:** Mark 15:33; Luke 23:44, 45

This coming week we are going to have something very special happen in our world. Does anyone know what it is?

*(Some of the children will know that an eclipse is expected.)*

Yes, we are going to see an eclipse. The moon will pass in between the sun and the earth. It will start to happen about five in the afternoon. By six, we will notice that it is darker, even though it is still daytime. Then, by seven, it will be over. It is a natural event, and it will be a lot of fun to watch.

You won't be able to look at it, because it would really hurt your eyes if you tried to look at the sun. You wouldn't be able to see anything anyway; it would just be too bright. So, I'll show you how to use this.

*(The account of Jesus' dying is almost always presented, especially to children, in tandem with the account of his rising again. This is as it should be; the resurrection is the point of it all, the wonderful news, the hope of humanity. However, it seemed of value to point out that it was a terrible thing for Jesus to die, terrible in God's sight and reflected in the natural world. These children hear that Jesus lives; let them think for a bit that he truly died.)*

I made a hole in this sheet of paper. I'll hold it like this [*parallel to the ground, tilted in the direction of the sun*] so that the sun will shine through. The shadow of the moon crossing the path of the sun will show on the ground underneath and I can watch it this way.

*(The demonstration is for the parents as well as the children. They will remember and know how to help their child to use the paper to track the eclipse.)*

But there was a day when the sun grew dark, and it stayed that way for three hours. It was really dark, like at night. It was the day that Jesus was crucified. They nailed him to a cross so that he would die. It took a long time, and while it was happening, the light from the sun was darkened. The whole world grew dark. People knew that something was very wrong.

Jesus was dying. He was the Light of the World and he was dying.

So when you see the eclipse on Wednesday, you will know that it is just something natural, something wonderful, in God's creation. But when you see it, think about the day when Jesus was dying, and the whole world got dark.

*(The meteorologist in our community tells me that three hours of darkness is much longer than any natural eclipse would last. It is he who suggested the paper with the pinhole.)*

# 18

## Gateways

**Opportunity:** Anytime.

**Materials:** None.

**Point:** There is one specific way to come to God.

**Scripture:** John 10:7, 9:

> Jesus said again, "I tell you the truth, I am the gate for the sheep...I am the gate; whoever enters through me will be saved...."

Matthew 7:13,14:

> "Enter through the narrow gate. For wide is the gate and broad is the road that leads to destruction, and many enter through it. But small is the gate and narrow the road that leads to life, and only a few find it."

I was out walking this week, with my family. We went down a narrow road that leads between some fields. We passed near where our neighbors pasture their horses. After a while, the road stopped and there were only the fields, with stone walls around them. The farmer had made a place in the wall where he had put part of a steel drum, laid on its side. The farmer's dog could go through there, but the cow or the horse could not.

We just moved it easily and went through the little place where it had been. Then we replaced it carefully.

(*Be sure to observe the local rules of law and etiquette concerning private lands and gates and fences. If someone has given you permission to pass through, mention that. Use whatever narrow entries are present in your area. It might be the gate in a schoolyard or a tennis court as well as a farmer's pasture. Where we live, it is considered perfectly reasonable to walk through an empty field as long as it is left undisturbed.*)

There was only one narrow place in the wall where we could pass through. The Bible says that if anyone wants to come to God, it is like that; they may come, but there is only *one way*.

If we had not gone through the farmer's little gate, we could not have gone on. If we do not go through God's only gate, we cannot go on to him either. Do you know what that way is?

It is the Lord Jesus Christ. It is the fact that he died for us and rose to life again. When we trust him, we can come to God. We can belong to God. Jesus himself is our door, our gate to God. He is the only one.

Let's pray:

''Lord Jesus, you are the way to everlasting life. Thank you for loving us and coming to die and to rise from death. We trust you to bring us close to God our heavenly Father. *Amen.*''

51

# 19

## Rules

**Opportunity:** Anytime, but the beginning of the school year is a time for many children to think about rules.

**Point:** Jesus' rule was "Love the LORD with all your heart and love you neighbor as you love yourself."

**Materials:** Something with a rule written on it—a sign or a notice. There are lots of these around. Mine came from the local elementary school where a class had written out some rules and posted them on a bulletin board. Signs such as DO NOT ENTER and NO SMOKING are easy to find, easy to borrow. Resist borrowing any stop signs, unless you want to make a bright copy of your own!

**Scripture:** Matthew 22:37, 39

I was in the elementary school this week, and I saw these rules on a bulletin board. The principal, Mr. Brown, said that I could borrow them today. Have you seen these rules?

(*Read the rules*.) NO RUNNING IN THE HALLS. NO WRITING ON THE WALLS.

What are some other rules we use?

"Look both ways before you cross the street" . . . "No smoking" . . . "Keep your hands to yourself."

When Jesus was on earth, they had so many rules that you had to think about it all the time. There were rules like, Don't eat certain things; don't walk too far or carry anything heavy on the Sabbath, and then there were the rules we still have, such as no lying, no stealing, no killing.

Now people could see that Jesus was a good man. They could see that he loved God's law, so one time they asked him:

"Teacher, what is the greatest commandment, or rule?"

They thought that he might not be able to answer such a difficult question. But Jesus could answer it, all right. Do you know what he said?

(*Some of them may know. If they do, let them tell, and then reinforce the statement by repeating it yourself*.)

Jesus told them that it is (not *was*, *is*):

"Love the LORD your God with all your heart and with all your soul and with all your mind. This is the first and greatest commandment. And the second is like it: Love your neighbor as yourself."

That's easy to remember: "Love the Lord your God" and "Love the people around you."

(*Have the children repeat it with you*.)

Let's pray:

"Lord, we love you and we thank you for loving us. Help us to obey your good laws. Help us to love each other, for Jesus' sake. *Amen*."

# 20

## Washing Up

**Opportunity:** Anytime.

**Point:** We need to ask for forgiveness of sin daily, but Jesus saves us from the *power* of sin once and for all. (It sounds difficult and theological put this way, but put in the way that Jesus described it to Peter and the way you can present it to the children, it is easy to understand.)

**Materials:** A plastic bag, or a small basket, with a towel, a washcloth, and a bar of soap inside.

**Scripture:** John 13:1–17

I have a washcloth here and some soap and a towel. Yesterday I was pulling weeds in my garden. My hands got all dirty, and when I came inside, I had to use a lot of soap to get them clean.

Couldn't I just leave my hands dirty?

("No.")

Why not?

("It doesn't feel good" . . . "Everything you touch would get dirty.")

Right. Jesus said we are like that in our hearts too. When we give our lives to Jesus, he makes us clean from all the things we have done wrong and thought wrong. But then, some time goes by. Maybe you are mean to somebody—or your mom asks you if you picked up your stuff, and you say yes but you really didn't. Maybe you lock your little brother out of the house. I did that once when I was little. We need to be clean again, inside ourselves. We need to ask Jesus to forgive and to change whatever it is that is wrong. We still belong to him, but we need to 'wash up.' Do you know what I'm talking about?

Let's pray right now and ask Jesus to do that.

"Lord, you know about whatever anyone here has done or thought that is wrong. You can make us clean, from big things that are wrong and from little things that are wrong, too. We ask you to do that now and we thank you.

In Jesus' name. *Amen.*"

*(Check the children's faces as you ask if they understand. You will see that many of them know exactly what you are talking about. They need the reassurance that falling short of the Christian walk is a common human experience and that there is immediate help for anyone who sins. Children need a model to know how to pray for forgiveness. Your prayer with them can be that model.)*

# 21

## Stethoscopes

**Opportunity:** Anytime.

**Point:** God is working in our lives all the time, but sometimes we have to listen in a very quiet and special way.

**Materials:** A stethoscope. A real one is best and can sometimes be borrowed from an interested doctor, nurse, or veterinarian.

**Scripture:** Psalm 46:10

Do you know what this is?

("A stethoscope"..."A thing to listen to your heart.")

Have you had someone listen to your heart with one of these? Would you like to try it?

You have to be really quiet. Is your dress making a sound? Let's try it on a T-shirt.

(*Let one child try it and assure the others they will have a chance later.*)

Okay. What do you hear? (*Motion for everyone to be very still.*)

("My heart is beating.")

Yes, it's just pumping away. The stethoscope makes the sound louder, but you still have to be very quiet to hear it.

Listening to God is just that way. When we pray, we talk to God, and we also listen, but we have to listen in a very quiet way. What's a good way to do that?

("At night, before you go to sleep" . . . "Outdoors, by yourself.")

Yes, those are good times. Do I have to be alone to use this stethoscope?

("No.")

I just have to decide to get real quiet and listen. That's what we can do when we listen to God. Let's do that now, not with the stethoscope but with the part of ourselves that listens to God.

"Lord Jesus, you are here, and we are just going to be quiet and listen to your presence."

(*Wait a few moments and then add,* "Amen.")

(*Be sure to go out with the children so that you can give the rest of them the opportunity to listen through the stethoscope.*)

# 22

## Cold Through and Through

**Opportunity:** Very cold weather.

**Point:** God can change a cold and angry person to a warm-hearted one.

**Materials:** None.

**Scripture:** Ezekiel 11:19, 20

Have any of you been really cold lately? I see Danielle has a furry coat on, and Gina is wearing her boots. It has been really cold around here lately, and we have all been finding ways to keep warm.

The Bible says that sometimes people feel cold and hard in their hearts, not the heart that pumps your blood, but the part of you that loves and feels things for other people. When someone is feeling cold-hearted, they are mad at everybody and they don't care about anybody else. They don't even care about God. They don't want to be hugged or even touched.

("Not even by their mothers and fathers.")

Sometimes people feel like that. What can you do? Would a coat help?

("No.")

The Bible says that when we turn to God and ask him, he will give us a warm heart full of love. We have to ask him and we have to want to follow his ways.

So, even when it's freezing outside, God will give us warm hearts on the inside. What's a good way to share your warm heart with someone else? You can give them a hug!

(*Here, give hugs to anyone who looks as if he/she would like one. Follow the children out to make sure you don't miss anyone. It is a sad thing to be left out of warm-hearted hugging because you are shy or a little slow to respond.*)

# 23

## Afraid of the Dark

**Opportunity:** Anytime.

**Point:** God, our loving Lord, is present in the darkness.

**Materials:** None.

**Scripture:** Psalm 121:3; Psalm 139:12

$A$nybody here ever wake up in the middle of the night and feel scared?

(*Let one or two children share. They will want to give more responses than time will allow. Just say,* "You can tell me a little later," *and move on.*)

Robin is afraid when she hears noises, and Billy is afraid when he's camping, and he's out in the woods. It happens when it's really dark and you are all alone, or maybe the only one awake—right? What do you do to make it better?

("I turn on the light" . . . "I wake my sister up" . . . "I go and get in bed with my parents.")

How many of you go and get in bed with somebody else? That makes it all right, doesn't it? Is it fun to be out in the woods in the dark when your dad is awake, Billy?

("Yes, I feel safe then.")

The Bible says that the darkness is just like the light to God. He knows what's in the corners and under the bed. It's not a surprise to him. The Bible also says that the Lord watches over us and does not sleep.

Here, I'll show you.

(*Open your Bible to Psalm 121:3.*)

. . . he who watches over you will not slumber;
Indeed, he who watches over Israel [that means all those God loves]
    will neither slumber nor sleep.

So, the next time you feel nervous in the dark, remember who is there with you!

("God is there" . . . "I could say, 'Good night, God.'")

Let's pray:

"Lord, you are with us in the darkness, you are with us in the light. When we think we are alone, you are there beside us. Thank you, Lord. In Jesus' name we pray. *Amen.*"

# 24

## String Beans: A Gift of Something Living

**Opportunity:** Anytime, but especially just before Easter.

**Point:** God begins a new life in us when we respond to Jesus.

**Materials:** A packet of string beans. (These are large enough to keep track of, and they are sure to sprout if given a little soil, water, and light. They grow into a vigorous vine. Plan enough to give each child two.)

**Scripture:** John 12:23, 24

It was a sad time for Jesus. He told his friends,

''The hour has come . . . I tell you the truth, unless a kernel of wheat falls to the ground and dies, it remains only a single seed. But if it dies, it produces many seeds.''

His friends didn't know what he was talking about.

Do you know? He was talking about getting ready to die. He knew that he would come to life again, but still, it was hard. He was telling his friends that if he died and came to life again, he would be able to start some of his life in each of us!

And that's what happened. Jesus died, but God made him alive again. Now when you start to trust in Jesus, it's like a seed, so small and hidden you wonder if it's real. But after a while, the seed that Jesus gives you grows into life that helps you love people and that will last forever.

I'm going to give you two string-bean seeds. They will grow into a string-bean vine because that's what kind of seed they are. You can bury it in a little dirt in a cup or a pot, about an inch deep, and give it a little water and lots of sunshine. After a while these hard little seeds will become living plants, just like the little seed of faith, planted deep in our hearts, grows into Jesus' life in us.

(*Give each child two string-bean seeds to take with them.*)

# 25

## Long-Distance Runners

**Opportunity:** When someone in the congregation is in a race. It may be a high-school track meet, a community fun run, or a full-fledged marathon. Adjust the details of the story to reflect the realities of your situation.

**Point:** A runner puts everything aside in order to run a race. So does a Christian, to follow the Lord.

**Materials:** A pair of worn running shoes.

**Scripture:** Hebrews 12:1, 2

I've brought something really special with me today; a pair of running shoes. Tom wore these when he ran in the marathon last week. They're dirty around the toes, and the bottoms are all worn and pressed down. Tom looked kind of worn-out himself when the race was over. They ran all the way from Folsom, down to the Capitol building. The finish line was right in front of that big white building with the gold dome.

("Did he win the race?")

Everyone who finished was a winner. They had to run *so* far. All the runners were so tired when they finished. Some of them could hardly stand up. How could they run that far?

Well, Tom kept his eyes on his goal; he wanted to run that race, all the way! He practiced by running every day. He ate foods that were good for him—no ice cream! He did everything he could to become a good runner.

On the day of the race, when he got tired, he just kept going. When he got thirsty, he just kept on running. After a while, his legs started to hurt—a lot—but he knew the finish line was up ahead, and he kept running until he crossed it!

The Bible says that sometimes it is hard to live God's way. Sometimes it's really hard. Then we need to keep our eyes on Jesus. Remember, like a good runner, just keep going.

# 26

## Best Friends

**Opportunity:** Anytime a friend has helped someone finish a difficult project.

**Point:** A friend can help a person achieve something difficult. We do it for each other, and the Holy Spirit does it for us. This illustration involves completing a race, but the occasion could be a building project or any other great effort.

**Materials:** None.

**Scripture:** John 14:25–27

Last week I told you about a race. I brought the running shoes. Today I want to tell you about a friend. Do you have a really good friend?

("Amanda is my best friend"..."And Abigail is mine.")

Well, Tom, the person who ran the long race, has a best friend named John. Sometimes John ran with

Tom. They talked about the race. They knew it would be so hard that Tom might not be able to finish it. So John decided to help him. He put on his running clothes, and he drove to a spot near the end of the race. John watched for Tom. When he saw him coming, running kind of slow, John jumped into the race and ran along beside him. Tom was so tired. He had been running for more than two hours, but he was glad to see his friend.

John said, "You can make it, Tom," and he ran beside him all the way to the end of the race.

That is the way a friend helps another. And that is the way the Bible says the Holy Spirit helps us, whether it is running a race, learning how to read, or trying to tie our shoes, the Holy Spirit will help us if we ask him.

# 27

## Plumb Line

**Opportunity:** Anytime, but especially if any building is going on.

**Point:** A godly person is a measure of Christian reality in a distorted world.

**Materials:** A plumb line. This is the ancient tool mentioned by the prophet Amos and still in use today. It can be found at a hardware store or among the tools of any builder. A carpenter's level may also be used.

**Scripture:** Amos 7:7, 8

Anybody know what this is? It's a plumb line and a plumb bob. You hold it up to see if a wall or a post is straight. Builders use it.

(*Before the service, look for one or two things to measure that won't require much moving around on the part of the children. A pulpit or communion table is usually convenient.*)

Let's see. Is this straight? Yes, it is.

The Bible says that we who follow God's ways are like this plumb line; we show God's yardstick in a world that isn't quite right.

Let's see. What happens if someone shoves someone else at school?

("They shove back.")

What is God's way?

("You should be kind to them" . . . "You could say to stop it but you shouldn't be mean to them.")

Yes, that's exactly right; you could say to stop it but you shouldn't be mean to them. God's ways are better. And God's people show his ways, just like the plumb line shows what a straight line really is.

Let's go measure the tables in the Sunday-school room!

# 28

## Cheering

**Opportunity:** Whenever there is a ball game or a race involving members of the congregation.

**Point:** We are surrounded by a cloud of witnesses.

**Materials:** Any program, pennant, pom-poms, baseball mitt, other.

**Scripture:** Hebrews 12:1

I've been to two special places this week. I brought this back from one of them.

(*Bring the baseball mitt or the pennant out of the bag.*)

This is Pete's glove. He's been playing baseball, and his team won last week. Eric, your brothers play baseball too, don't they? Do you ever go and cheer for them?

("We all go. My whole family cheers for them.")

I love to watch Pete play. When he crosses home plate, we really yell. I've been to the hospital this week too. Gina's mother has been sick, and it's hard for her right now. We prayed for her this morning. She's struggling hard to get well. She's working as hard to get well as Pete works to win a baseball game, and we cheer for her, too. Do you know how we cheer for her?

("When we go to see her?" . . . "When we send her cards?")

Yes, we're cheering for her then. We're saying, "Come on, we know you can do it." But we also cheer for her—we help her along—when we pray for her.

The Bible says that we are surrounded by a "cloud of witnesses." We can't see them, but they are cheering for us because we are part of God's family—part of his team.

(*Perhaps you will want to pray for the person you have mentioned at this point. If it is someone the children know they will experience being a ministering, a "cheering," part of the Christian family. If it is someone unknown to them, it will lack that flavor of reality. Be sure to check, if you need to, with the person or the family involved.*)

"Father, we pray for Gina's mother today. Help her to get better. Help her to keep on doing the things that make her well. Help her not to get tired or discouraged.

We pray in Jesus' name. *Amen.*"

# 29

## Emmanuel, or, Will God Be In Turkey?

**Opportunity:** Advent or when a child is moving.

**Point:** One of Jesus' names is "God With Us."

**Materials:** None.

**Scripture:** Isaiah 7:14 (paraphrased)

Where is God? Anyone have any ideas? ("God is here" . . . "God is up in heaven" . . . "God is in my heart.")

Jessica and Jeffrey are going to move to Incirlik, a city in Turkey. Do you think God will be there?

("Yes, God is everywhere.")

Sometimes it's a little scary to think about God because he is so big, so great. It's hard to imagine, isn't it?

Well, God made a promise long before Jesus was born. He said:

"Behold!

"A virgin [a young woman] will be with child and will give birth to a son and will call him Emmanuel."

That name means, "God with us" and that is Jesus' name. "Emmanuel: God, who is right here with us."

When Jeffrey and Jessica get to Incirlik, Jesus will be there too, just as he is here. Does that help a little bit?

*(Jessica and Jeffrey did move to Incirlik. However, to young children, St. Louis or San Diego may seem just as strange. They need to know the Lord is there, just as he is in the place that has been home.)*

# 30

## The Man Who Couldn't Believe

**Opportunity:** After Easter.

**Point:** Jesus really died. Jesus really lives again.

**Materials:** Hammer, nail, small board.

**Scripture:** John 20:24–30

Last week was Easter. What special thing happened at Easter?

("Jesus rose from the dead.")

Yes, Jesus rose from the dead. Isn't that amazing? Did you ever hear of anyone else who was really dead and then became alive again? It's hard to imagine.

(*At this point, hammer the nail into the wood. Make no comment, but wiggle the nail around and pull it out again. Make sure you have a good-sized hole.*)

Jesus had a friend and follower who had a hard time

believing that he rose from the dead. The man's name was Thomas. He loved Jesus but he could not imagine that someone who had died could be alive again. The other disciples told him that they had seen Jesus, but Thomas said:

"Unless I see the nail marks in his hands and put my finger where the nails were . . . I will not believe it." And he didn't.

A week later, Thomas and some of Jesus' other friends were in a house. The doors were locked, but suddenly, there was Jesus! He said to Thomas:

"Put your finger here; see my hands . . . Stop doubting and believe."

(*Hold up the board and touch the nail hole. Let any child who reaches out, touch it also.*)

A man's hand is much softer than this wood. The nails made holes all the way through. Thomas saw the holes, and he looked at Jesus' face, and he knew it was all true; Jesus had really been dead and now he was really alive!

He said, "My Lord and my God!"

Then Jesus said something about you and me and other people like us. He said, "Thomas, you are blessed because you have seen me. Those who have not seen my hands like you have and still believe are blessed too." And that is you and me!

# 31

## Gone Fishing

**Opportunity:** One of the Sundays after Easter.

**Point:** After the excitement was over, Jesus was still there, just as he is here, now.

**Materials:** Fishing line, hook or net, large enough to see easily but small enough to hold conveniently.

**Scripture:** John 21:1–14

What did you do the day after Easter? ("I went back to school" . . . "Nothing.")

I went back to work, just like I do every Monday. It was a pretty ordinary day.

After Jesus rose from the dead, his followers didn't quite know what to do. After a while, they went back to work, too. They went fishing, because that was their job. They went out at night in a boat with nets. All night they pulled the nets through the water, just as they had always done, but they didn't catch anything at all.

When morning came, they saw someone standing on the shore.

He called to them, "Catch any fish?"

And of course they hadn't. Then he said, "Throw your net on the right side of the boat, and you will find some."

So they did, and they caught so many fish they couldn't haul the net in. Then someone realized that it was Jesus standing there. Peter jumped into the water and swam to meet him.

Jesus was there waiting for them. He had built a fire and was cooking some fish for them and some bread. Jesus was really alive, and he was there with them. He is here with us, too.

Let's pray:

"Lord, Easter is over. We are all back at school. Help us to know that you are with us here and at school. Help us to realize that you are alive and you are with us wherever we go. *Amen.*"

# 32

## Children of Light

**Opportunity:** Anytime.

**Point:** We are children of light when we belong to Jesus, the Light of the World.

**Materials:** An X-ray photograph. Sometimes a doctor, veterinarian, or X-ray technician will give you a discarded one (with the identifying names cut off). It doesn't have to be your own. You will also need a flashlight. Be sure the batteries are strong.

**Scripture:** John 8:12; Ephesians 5:8–20

I brought two things today. Can you hold this envelope for me, Eric?

Did you know you can hold a flashlight up against your fingers, and it will shine through your flesh? Hold up your hand, and I'll show you.

(*Hold the flashlight tight against the child's hand. The light will pass through in a pink glow.*)

Here is a picture of a light that shone all the way through somebody's shoulder. You can see the bones.

("It's an X-ray" . . . "I had one of those.")

(*If the children don't name the X-ray, mention what it is. Probably, they will tell you.*)

Jesus is called the Light of the World. When we belong to him, we have his light inside us. It shines through, just like this flashlight. (*Shine the flashlight against another child's hand.*)

The light is not a flashlight kind of light though. Do you know what it might be? It's more like a kind of love, God's love for us and our love for other people. The Bible says that we belong to the light. It shines right through us. It helps us love people just like Jesus loves them.

# 33

## Roots that Go Deep

**Opportunity:** Anytime.

**Point:** We are created to know God, and we grow to our full potential only when we live in relationship with him.

**Materials:** A bonsai or other dwarfed plant.

**Scripture:** Ephesians 3:17–19

I brought this little tree with me. It looks like the big pine out by the Sunday-school building. It is the same kind exactly, but this tree will never grow any taller than it is now. Someone cut the main root. The smaller roots are still there, and it will live for a long time, but it will always be small enough to grow in a dish. It was meant to have a deep root, and now that root is gone.

People are like that too. We are meant to let our love for God and our trust in him grow deep and strong, like the root of a tree. If we decide *not* to do that, we will still live, but we won't become all that God meant us to be.

The Bible says that we can have deep roots in God's love. Then we will be able to know how "wide and . . . high and deep . . ." Christ's love is and grow into all that he has planned for us!

Let's pray:

"Dear Jesus, I know that you love me very much. I want to love you too. I want to grow to be everything you want me to be. *Amen.*"

(*This is an abstract idea; not all the children will grasp it. But some children will understand it perfectly well, and know they have a choice to make.*)

# 34

## Jobs

**Opportunity:** Anytime there is a job for a child to do to help an adult. Christmas offers the opportunity to make cookies. There are other occasions when a child can be of real help to an adult; when leaves need to be raked or the dog needs to be bathed. Watch for one that fits your life.

**Point:** God promises important work for his children.

**Materials:** Possibly none. In this case I brought a couple of cookie cutters.

**Scripture:** Ephesians 2:10

I made some Christmas cookies this week, and I invited Ginger and Jennifer and Jason and Jessica to come over and help me. We made a lot of cookies. It was going to be a lot of work for me, and I really needed their help. We rolled out the dough and cut out the cookies, and after they baked, we put frosting on them. We all worked hard, didn't we? And we had fun!

Have you ever helped an adult with some kind of work?

("I help my dad wash the dog"..."I help my grandmother water her plants.")

Are you a good dogwasher, Kelly?

("Yes. I know how to hold him so he doesn't shake.")

The Bible says that God is working on us, helping us to be the special people that he planned. The Bible also says that he has planned for us to do some good and important things for him, some "work." He plans jobs for us, just like I planned for Jason and his sisters to help me with the cookies. Isn't that exciting? Don't you wonder what he has planned for you?

*(Let the children make a few responses but don't try to "answer" the question. That is a discovery they will have to make as they grow. To open the possibility is your goal today.)*

# 35

## Targets

**Opportunity:** Anytime, but especially when someone is learning a sport.

**Point:** Fix your eyes on Jesus.

**Materials:** A target or a small basketball hoop.

**Scripture:** Hebrews 12:1–3

J oey, I heard that your father is teaching you to play basketball. Am I right? [*Hold up the small hoop.*] (''Yes. He's teaching me to shoot baskets.'')

How do you do that? Did he lower the hoop?

(''He set up a little hoop for me in the backyard. I just go out and practice shooting baskets.'')

Joey has to fix his eyes on the hoop and then carefully throw the ball so that it goes right in. He probably has to practice over and over. Right, Joey?

(''Right. Sometimes my dad shows me how to do it.'')

*(The child will probably mention that his dad or brother shows him how to play. If not, mention this yourself.)*

It's important to watch your dad to see the right way to do it. The Bible says that we need to "fix our eyes on Jesus" just like a target. He will show us how to live the way we need to; how to be strong and loving people. Sometimes it's hard to be a Christian; it's a lot like basketball; we have to keep our eyes on the target (that's Jesus) and keep practicing.

# 36

## Someone's Knocking
## at the Door

**Opportunity:** Around Halloween. Many Christian fami-
lies do not participate in trick-or-treat or any Halloween activity. You may want to say that the children
will go only to houses where they have friends, or that
they don't go at all. In either case, someone probably
knocks at *your* door and that is the opportunity.

**Point:** Christ "knocks at the door" and waits for us to let
him in.

**Materials:** A Bible, with a marker at the third chapter of
Revelation

**Scripture:** Revelation 3:20 (RSV)

Tomorrow is Halloween. Some children will
get dressed up and go trick-or-treating. Some don't
do that. The children who live next door to me will
come and knock on my door. I'll hear their voices

outside. They will be hoping that I'll answer. Do you think I should open the door?

Well, I will. I'll invite them in so that I can see their costumes, and I'll give them some peanuts for a treat. My door is unlocked, but they would never open it. They would wait for me.

Jesus says [*here open the Bible to the reference*]:

"Behold, I stand at the door and knock; if anyone hears my voice and opens the door, I will come to him [or her] and eat with him and he with me."

Jesus waits until we hear his voice and know that he is there. He knocks, and waits until we invite him to come in.

Would any one of you like to invite Jesus to come into your life?

(*You will be able to see an alert interest, a responsiveness, if any child is ready to take this step. If there is, move on to a prayer to receive Christ. If not, end in this way:*)

Jesus wants to be part of your lives, but he will always wait until you invite him in. And you can do that anytime you like.

(*Halloween is a time of anxiety and uncertainty for many children. It is supposed to be "fun" but often has a threatening quality as well. What wonderful reality we have to offer instead: Christ is present in our world and wants to be part of our lives. He knocks and waits, leaving to us the great honor of choosing him!*)

# 37

## Bugs

**Opportunity:** Mild weather, when you can find sow bugs under a rock or board. Bug must curl up when touched!

**Point:** God became a man in order to show us his love.

**Materials:** A small box containing a couple of bugs.

**Scripture:** John 1:14

(*Open the box slowly.*)


I have some bugs here. I found them under a rock in my backyard.

(*Let the children peer into the box and touch the bugs if they like.*)

They roll up in little balls if you touch them. They are afraid. They want to be left alone, in a dark place.

How can I show them that I won't hurt them?

("Give them food" . . . "Put them back under their rock" . . . "Make a little house for them.")

Well, I did make a little house for them but I don't think they like it very much. "Hey little bugs, I won't hurt you!" Do you think that helped?

("They can't understand you.")

No, they can't understand me. What if I wanted them to know I really cared about them, even loved them?

("They just couldn't understand you.")

What if I could become little, just like them? What if I became that kind of bug? Then could they understand?

We are much more than bugs! But God did that for us! He is so great. It's hard for us to understand him because he is so much more than we are. So he became just like us. He became a baby, like Mary Ann's new sister, and then a little child, like Mary Ann and William. He became a person living in this world so that he could show us that he loves us!

# 38

## Getting Ready for a Guest

**Opportunity:** Whenever you or someone known to the children is getting ready for someone to come and stay with them; a new baby, a grandparent, or a guest.

**Point:** Just as we prepare a room so the new family member or guest will be pleased and feel at home, so Jesus prepares a place for us.

**Materials:** Something from the preparations—a piece of wallpaper, some paint-sample cards, or a bit of fabric.

**Scripture:** John 14:1–3

The grandma in our family is coming to visit, and we are getting ready for her. We put up some new wallpaper [*hold up the sample*]. We vacuumed the carpet and we put clean sheets on the bed. I put a book on the table that I thought she might like to read at night, if she couldn't fall asleep, and we put a bowl of flowers there too. I think she will like it.

*(Adjust this part to the reality of your experience. Sometimes it is a new baby who is expected and prepared for with a crib and stuffed animals, or a sick relative who needs special equipment.)*

Have you ever fixed a room for someone who is coming to your house?

("Yes. We had to put a pitcher of water out for my grandpa so he could take his pills at night" . . . "We get extra blankets out.")

It's fun to make a room special for a person.

That is just what Jesus told his friends he was doing. He was about to die, and they were afraid. They didn't want him to leave—and especially not to die—and they didn't want to die themselves.

But Jesus told them this,

*(Open your Bible to John 14 and read verses 1–3. Practice ahead of time so that the words are familiar.)*

He is fixing a special place, a room that we will like, in God's house. He promised that he would do that and that he would come back sometime and take us there with him! Wow!

# 39

## The Peach Tree's Secret

**Opportunity:** Whenever you have access to a fruit still attached to its vine or branch.

**Point:** The fruit is a part of the living plant. We are a part of Christ.

**Materials:** Fruit, still attached to a bit of branch or vine. Grapes, peaches, apples, cherries, all work.

**Scripture:** John 15:1–17

We have a peach tree in our front yard. It's not much of a tree, kind of skinny and bare all winter. In the summer it gets a few leaves. But every July, it turns into something special, and you can see why we keep it. It has big ripe peaches then, and they are delicious—so sweet and juicy that they drip all over your chin! I brought one today. It's still on its branch.

The peach didn't get that way all by itself. It had to

be part of the peach tree. It shows what that skinny little tree is really like.

Jesus said that when we belong to him, we are like the peach on the branch; we are part of him. This fruit is so peachy because it is part of the peach tree. We grow to be like Jesus because we are part of him.

Let's pray:

"Lord Jesus, we are glad that we can be a part of you. We want to live close to you and grow to be like you. Please help us to do that. *Amen.*"

# 40

## A Bridge to God

**Opportunity:** Anytime.

**Point:** There is only one way to reach God the Father, and that is through his Son, Jesus Christ.

**Materials:** None, but you will need to identify a bridge that the children have crossed, either on foot or in a car.

**Scripture:** John 14:6, 7

Have you gone over the bridge in the park? I walked over it the other day with Nancy. It's really high. You can see the rocks and the water way down below. Nancy was afraid to walk across it, but it's the only way you can get to the part of the park where she wanted to go.

(''My mother makes me hold her hand when we cross that bridge.'')

Yes, I know several people who are very careful

when they cross that bridge. What would happen if you tried to go around it instead?

("You couldn't"..."You would have to climb down to the river and try to get across the water"... "You would probably fall and hurt yourself on the rocks.")

You really could not get across to the other side, could you? (Or if you could, your baby sister or your grandmother could not.) So if you want to go to that part of the park, you have to go across the bridge. You have to trust that it will hold you all the way across.

Jesus said: "I am the way, the truth, and the life. No one comes to the Father except through me. If you really knew me, you would know my Father as well."

Jesus is our bridge. When we know him, we know God. We can count on him for that. There isn't any other way.

Let's pray:

"Jesus, you are our bridge to God. We can safely count on you. Thank you for bringing us to God. *Amen.*"

# 41

## Yo-yos

**Opportunity:** Anytime you have mastered a few tricks with a yo-yo.

**Point:** Once we choose to follow Jesus, we belong to him forever.

**Materials:** A yo-yo.

**Scripture:** 1 Peter 1:3–5

*(You will need to practice for this, so that you can tell your story at the same time you spin the yo-yo out and back again. Seat the children in front of you and then start speaking.)*

I have to stand up to do this. Move a little so I won't hit you with my yo-yo.

*(Do one short trick with the yo-yo.)*

This yo-yo goes all the way out to the end of the string, and it looks like it stops. Then it comes up again. I can control when it goes down and when it comes up.

When we decide to follow Jesus, he makes us his own children forever. Sometimes it feels like we're far away [*spin the yo-yo out*] but we still belong to him, and pretty soon, it feels as if we're close to him again.

(*Spin the yo-yo back, if you haven't already.*)

Out and back, near and far, we still belong to him. He still has hold of us, just like I still have hold of the yo-yo, even when it's clear at the end of the string.

Now I'll put the yo-yo away and let's pray:

"Lord Jesus, thank you that we belong to you forever, and that you are in control of our lives when we ask you to be. *Amen.*"

# 42

## Running to Meet Him

**Opportunity:** Anytime.

**Point:** We really will see Jesus.

**Materials:** A telephone.

**Scripture:** 1 Corinthians 13:12; Revelation 22:4; John 6:37

This week we talked on the telephone to our uncle. We talk to him every so often, but we haven't seen him for a long time. Next week he's coming. We can hardly wait to see his face.

Have you ever talked to someone on the phone and then, after a long time, actually gotten to see that person?

("Yes, my dad when he was away"..."My grandpa.")

Someday I will see Jesus. I will look at his face. So will you. What do you think you will do?

(*Give the children just a moment here. You will do more later.*)

I think I might be shy. My son Paul said:

"Mommy, do you know what I will do when I see Jesus? I will go running to meet him."

Each of us will really see Jesus someday. What will *you* do?

(*Give each child who wants to, an opportunity to reply. This is a risky endeavor. It should not be attempted until the children trust you, and you know that they are sure that Jesus welcomes little children. Then give them this chance to consider; they will see Jesus!*)

The Bible has a promise for us. Jesus said, "Whoever comes to me I will never send away." Let's pray:

"Thank you, Jesus, that we are going to see you face to face. We can hardly wait! *Amen.*"

# 43

## Flashlights

**Opportunity:** Anytime.

**Point:** The Bible gives us direction for our lives.

**Materials:** Flashlight (Be sure to check that the batteries are strong.)

**Scripture:** Psalm 119:105

**D**o you ever use one of these?

(''Sure, it's a flashlight'' . . . ''I have one of those.'')

Several of you have flashlights. When do you use them?

(''We use them when the electricity goes out.'' . . . ''When we go camping.'')

(*If the children do not suggest occasions on which to use flashlights, suggest some yourself.*)

You need one whenever it's dark and you can't see where you're going. You need it so you won't trip over something or go the wrong way.

The Bible is like a flashlight. It shows us things we really need to know and we might miss by ourselves. It tells us that God really loves us. It tells us that we need to be sorry for our sins. It tells us that we need to act in a caring way toward other people. It tells us that Jesus came to be our Savior. We wouldn't know that if the Bible didn't tell us.

The more we know about what the Bible says, the easier it is to choose the right way to live. It is like a flashlight on the path in the dark.

# 44

## The Man Who Was Willing to Look Silly

**Opportunity:** Anytime.

**Point:** Finding Christ is more important than anything else, even more important than keeping one's dignity.

**Materials:** None, but you will need to find a person in the congregation who is well known to the children, who shows personal dignity, and who is also willing to let you use him or her for this example.

**Scripture:** Luke 19:1–10

$A$re any of you tree climbers?

("I climb trees all the time" . . . "My mom won't let me.")

I used to climb trees when I was a child, but I don't anymore. Have any of you ever seen Mr. Brown in a tree?

(*Giggles all around.*)

I haven't either. Do you think he would ever climb a tree in his good clothes?

("He would change to his jeans"..."He would never climb a tree at all.")

There was a man in Jesus' time who had a very important job. He lived in a nice house and he always wore nice clothes. He liked to look nice. When Jesus came through his town, he wanted to see him. He knew that people would push and shove. He knew they would never let him through, and he would never get to see Jesus.

So he found a tree beside the road where Jesus would walk.

Even though he was a grown-up, an important man, and even though he wore good clothes, he climbed up in the tree to wait for Jesus.

(*By this time the children know it is the story of Zacchaeus. Let them supply you with his name. They are sure to do so.*)

Jesus saw him in the tree, and you know what he did...?

("He told him to come down.")

Yes, he did, and then Jesus went to Zacchaeus' house.

When Zacchaeus was face to face with Jesus, he did a strange thing. He said that he was sorry for the cheating he had done. He promised to give back all that he had taken and more beside. Something was very bad in Zacchaeus' life, and he wanted to make it right.

Jesus was glad he did. He said:

"Today salvation has come to this house...For the Son of Man came to seek and to save what was lost."

Zaccheus was happy in his heart. It was worth climbing the tree, even in his good clothes.

*(This is a story known to many children as a game or a song. It is about an adult who set aside his dignity because of his need, and who gladly laid his cheating and acquisitive life at the feet of Jesus. I hope that identifying him with a real man of dignity and stature will help the children to see him as a person rather than a caricature.)*

# 45

## Dinner at Jesus' House

**Opportunity:** Around Thanksgiving or on Communion Sunday.

**Point:** Jesus had a special dinner with his friends. He promised that he would have a special meal with all of us someday.

**Materials:** A chunk of bread and a cup.

**Scripture:** Mark 14:12–26 (paraphrased)

Where did you have Thanksgiving dinner? ("At Grandma's house"..."At our house"... "With our friends.")

We all had dinner with people we love. That's what we do at Thanksgiving.

In Jesus' time, there was a special holiday when family and friends had dinner together. The Bible tells us about a special meal Jesus had with his friends. They rented a room and they had a feast of roast lamb and other delicious foods. But they had to do it in secret because some people were trying to arrest Jesus. It was just before he was killed. But that night they were all together, and it was sort of like Thanksgiving dinner.

(*Obviously Passover carries quite another message. The point here is that it was an important family and religious occasion.*)

They all had dinner and then Jesus took a chunk of bread and he gave thanks to God for all of it. Then he broke it up and passed it to his friends.

He said, "Take, eat. This is my body."

Then he took a cup of the wine they had and he passed it around and he said, "This is my blood and my new promise to you."

They were puzzled. They didn't know what he meant. They didn't know that Jesus was going to die. But Jesus knew. He was going to let it happen.

Then Jesus promised them, "I will not drink this until the day I drink it once again with you in my Father's kingdom."

("That's communion.")

Yes, that's what we remember when we have communion. It is so important that we ask children to wait until we are sure they understand it really well, and until we are sure they have accepted Christ as their Savior.

We are all waiting for that very special day, when we will sit at Jesus' table and have a very special dinner with him.

# 46

## The Charge Against Jesus

**Opportunity:** Before Holy Week.

**Point:** Jesus was charged with claiming to be the Son of God.

**Materials:** None.

**Scripture:** Matthew 26:62–66

Did you know that Jesus was arrested? Soldiers came and got him in the middle of the night, and they took him to jail.

He had to go before a judge. The judge asked him:

"Are you the Christ, the Son of God?"

Jesus said: "Yes, it is as you say . . . In the future you will see the Son of Man sitting at the right hand of the Mighty One and coming on the clouds of heaven."

When he heard that, the judge was so angry that he ripped his clothes. No one could say that! God was in heaven, and Jesus was a man! They didn't believe him, and they thought he was making fun of God! They were so angry that they decided he should die.

Was Jesus making fun of God? No, not at all! Why did Jesus say he was the Son of God?

("Because he really was.")

Exactly right! Because he really is the Son of God. He knew all those things would happen to him, even that they would really kill him. He let it happen because he loved his friends (and that includes us), and because he knew that he would conquer death and come to life again.

A lot of things were going on and some of them are hard to understand, but this part is very clear. Who did Jesus say he is?

("He is the Son of God.")

*(So much is contained in the story of Jesus' last week. You cannot possibly present all of it in the moments that are available and the children could not grasp it all if you could. The question, "Who is this Man?" is asked and answered here. It is enough for one Sunday morning!*

# 47

## What Do You Say when You're Squeezed?

**Opportunity:** Anytime.

**Point:** What we are inside shows up under pressure.

**Materials:** None.

**Scripture:** Matthew 12:33–37

We have a game we play with our dog. We squeeze him, very gently so that we don't hurt him, and he says, "Ummph!"

Have you ever been hugged like that—a tight hug, but careful, not scary? What do you say?

(*Be sure the distinction is there between loving squeezes and teasing, frightening ones.*)

There is a different kind of squeeze that's not so nice; when things go all wrong and you don't know what to do and you get mad. When that happens, sometimes I say, "Oh, rats!" and sometimes I say, "Please help me, Lord."

The Bible says this:

"Out of the overflow of the heart, the mouth speaks. The good [person] brings good things out of the good stored up in him, and the evil [person] brings evil . . ."

The next time you get caught in a bad spot, I wonder what you will say? If you are letting Jesus work in your heart, maybe you will say, "Rats!," or maybe "Ummph!" or maybe you'll say, "Please help me, Lord!"

Let's pray:

"Lord Jesus, we know that you love us and are there to help us when things go wrong. Thank you for that. It is so easy to love you back. It is so easy to ask you to help us whenever we have need. We pray in your great name. *Amen.*"

# 48

## Snapshots

**Opportunity:** When someone in the congregation is moving or going away for an extended time.

**Point:** We are of great value, to God and to each other.

**Materials:** A small camera, one that you can tuck unobtrusively in your pocket until you need it.

**Scripture:** Matthew 10:29–31

I'll be moving away soon. I will think about each one of you when I am gone and I'll remember your faces. I'll remember what is special about you; Claire's long pigtails and Suzanne's solemn smile and all the freckles on Burton's nose. You are important to me and I want to remember everything about you.

The memory of people's faces can get dim after a while, so I brought along a camera. After we go out to children's church, I'll take a picture of everyone.

*(Be sure to wait until you are outside to do this so that it won't detract from the worship service.)*

The Lord notices how you look, what you are like, because He loves you. He knows you so well that He knows how many hairs are growing on your head! He must be paying very close attention to you!

Let's thank God for loving us like that.

"Lord, it is good for us to be here with you. You see us, you notice everything about us because you love us. We love you too, and we praise you. We pray in Jesus' Holy Name. *Amen.*"

Now let's go take that picture. God sees your faces all the time, but I need some pictures!

# 49

## Somebody's Father

**Occasion:** The Sunday nearest Martin Luther King's birthday.

**Point:** Martin Luther King, Jr., was a man who trusted and obeyed God and who did something great in this country. He was also somebody's father and was making the world a better place for his children. Most children do not have a feeling for racism. Those I have told this story to have not understood more detailed explanations. They will hear these details as well as descriptions of his death for the rest of their lives. I want to tell them that he was a great and peaceful warrior and a loving father.

**Scripture:** Matthew 5:38,39:

> You have heard that it was said, "Eye for eye, and tooth for tooth." But I tell you, Do not resist an evil person. If someone strikes you on the right cheek, turn to him the other also.

I'm going to tell you about somebody's

father. He was a minister and he was a good dad. He taught his children that it was important to do the right thing. His name was Martin Luther King, Jr.

In our country there used to be some laws that made people feel bad. There were laws that said if your hair and your eyes and your skin were one color, you could not go to the same restaurants or amusement parks or even the same schools as other people.

Some people in Dr. King's church said,

"We don't like those laws. They are not right. What should we do?"

Martin Luther King tried to get the laws changed. He and some other people got together and held marches in the streets. They carried signs that said that everyone should have the same chances. They sat in restaurants that said they could not sit together if they were of different colors.

Sometimes Dr. King and his friends were arrested. What do you think his children thought? (*Give an opportunity for a response here. I have needed to assure children that he was not doing a bad thing, even if he was in jail.*)

His children knew that their dad listened to God and that he was in jail because he was doing the right thing.

Sometimes people hurt him and tried to get him to stop. But Martin Luther King trusted God. He knew God would help.

He thought about his children. He said:

> I have a dream
> that one day my four little children
> will be judged, not by the color of their skin,
> but by their character.

And that's what is beginning to happen. Some laws were changed; more laws need to be changed. It is important to treat people fairly, whatever the color of their skin and hair and eyes. Everyone should have the same opportunities and choices.

*(Of course this is a simplistic presentation of a most complex subject. Remember, the hearers are little children, from about 3 to 8. This is only one "bit" of information about a great man, but it is central.)*

# 50

## A Gift for Jesus

**Occasion:** Christmas or someone's birthday.

**Point:** We can give Jesus a very special gift: ourselves.

**Materials:** Birthday candles. (Make arrangements with those handling children's church to supervise the lighting of the candles.)

**Scripture:** Luke 2:1–7

Last week we had Christmas. Did you get a special gift? (*Wait for a few replies.*)

Did you know that you can give Jesus a very special gift?

Do you remember why God sent us his Son as a little baby? (*Wait for the answer that he would be our Savior, to save us from our sins.*)

Yes, Jesus did come to save us from our sins. In order for that to happen, we have to do something, too. We can give our hearts, the real part of us—inside—to Jesus.

This is how you do it. Tell God that you know that Jesus came because he loves you. Tell him that you know that sometimes there are bad feelings, bad ideas, inside and you would like him to take those away. Tell him that you want to give yourself to Jesus. That's it: a special gift for him.

*(Does this seem too simple? It is both simple and hard. The morning that I used this, Laura, a little girl of seven responded, "Oh, I want to do that. I want to give myself to Jesus." She was eager, even insistent. I walked her through the prayer again. She wasn't satisfied: "But I don't understand," she said, so I went out to children's church with her and talked with her there until she did understand.*

*This is a single-idea children's story. It depends on all the others you have told, as well as other teaching and preparation done by other loving Christians. If a child is ready, you will not really have* enough *time during the children's time to deal with him or her. Be ready to leave with the child and finish this important business in whatever time it will take.)*